KIDS AT WORK

LEWIS HINE

AND THE CRUSADE AGAINST CHILD LABOR

Newsboy, St. Louis, Missouri, 1910.

KIDS AT WORK

LEWIS HINE
AND THE CRUSADE AGAINST CHILD LABOR

BY RUSSELL FREEDMAN

WITH PHOTOGRAPHS BY LEWIS HINE

CLARION BOOKS   NEW YORK

Clarion Books
a Houghton Mifflin Harcourt Publishing Company imprint
3 Park Avenue, 19th Floor, New York, New York 10016
Text copyright © 1994 by Russell Freedman
Photographs by Lewis Hine

Type is 13-point Sabon.

Book design by Sylvia Frezzolini.

Manufactured in China

Library of Congress Cataloging-in-Publication Data

Freedman, Russell. Kids at work:
Lewis Hine and the crusade against child labor / Russell Freedman ;
with photographs by Lewis Hine.
p.   cm.
Includes bibliographical references and index.
ISBN 0-395-58703-4   PA ISBN 0-395-79726-8
1. Children—Employment—United States—History—Juvenile literature.
2. Hine, Lewis Wickes, 1874–1940—Juvenile literature.
3. Social reformers—United States—Biography—Juvenile literature.
4. Photographers—United States—Biography—
Juvenile literature. [Children—Employment.
2. Hine, Lewis Wickes, 1874–1940. 3. Social reformers.
4. Photographers.] I. Hine, Lewis Wickes, 1874–1940. II. Title.
HD6250.U3F67   1994   93-5989
331.3'1'092—dc20   CIP
[B]   AC

SCP 38 37 36 35 34 33 32
4500783685

For Phil Gerrard,
a kid at heart

Young Lewis Hine.

CONTENTS

Manuel, a five-year-old Mississippi shrimp-picker.

CHAPTER ONE

A CRUSADER WITH A CAMERA

Manuel is five years old but big for his age. When the whistle blows at 3 o'clock in the morning, he pulls on his clothes and hurries to the shrimp and oyster cannery where he spends the day peeling the shells off iced shrimp. He has been working as a shrimp-picker since he was four.

Manuel posed for his picture on a February morning in 1911 at a seafood cannery in Biloxi, Mississippi — a shrimp pail in each hand, a mountain of oyster shells behind his back. This spunky little boy was one of thousands of working children who were photographed by Lewis Hine in the years before the First World War.

America's army of child laborers had been growing steadily for the past century. The nation's economy was expanding. Factories, mines, and mills needed plenty of cheap labor. When Manuel's picture was taken, more than two million American children under sixteen years of age were a regular part of the work force. Many of them worked twelve hours or more a day, six days a week, for pitiful wages under unhealthy and hazardous conditions.

Thousands of young boys descended into dark and dangerous coal mines every day, or worked aboveground in the stifling dust of the coal breakers, picking slate from coal with torn and bleeding fingers. Small girls tended noisy machines in the spinning rooms of cotton mills, where the humid, lint-filled air made breathing difficult. They were kept awake by having cold water thrown in their faces. Three-year-olds could be found in the cotton fields, twelve-year-olds on factory night shifts. Across the country, children who should have been in school or at play had to work for a living.

By the early 1900s, many Americans were calling child labor "child slavery" and were demanding an end to it. They argued that long hours of work deprived children of an education and robbed them of their chance for a better future. Instead of preparing youngsters for useful lives as productive adults, child labor promised a future of illiteracy, poverty, and continuing misery.

Besides, the reformers said, children have certain rights. Above all, they have the right to be children and not breadwinners.

Lewis Hine, a New York City schoolteacher and photographer, was one of those early reformers. He knew that a picture can tell a powerful story. He felt so strongly about the use of children as industrial workers that he

Breaker boys at a Pennsylvania coal mine.

Spinner in a New England cotton mill, North Pownal, Vermont, 1910.

quit his teaching job to become an investigative photographer for the National Child Labor Committee (NCLC).

Hine traveled around the country with an old-fashioned box camera, taking pictures of kids at work. It took courage to get those pictures. Factory owners did not want photographers nosing around their plants, aiming cameras at underage workers. In the past, child-labor investigators had been harassed, jailed, and run out of town.

Hine was clever enough to bluff his way into many plants. He searched where he was not welcome, snapped scenes that were meant to be hidden from the public. At times, he was in real danger, risking physical attack when factory managers realized what he was up to. A slender, birdlike man who was usually retiring and shy, he put his life on the line in order to record a truthful picture of working children in early-twentieth-century America.

Seeing is believing, said Hine. If people could see for themselves the abuses and injustice of child labor, surely they would demand laws to end those evils. His pictures of sooty-faced boys in coal mines and small girls tending giant machines revealed a shocking reality that most Americans had never seen before.

*Little orphan,
Washington, D.C.,
1906.*

CHAPTER TWO

BECOMING A
PHOTOGRAPHER

A small-town boy from the Midwest, Lewis Wickes Hine grew up in Oshkosh, Wisconsin, where he was born on September 26, 1874. His parents ran a popular coffee shop and restaurant on Main Street. The family lived upstairs, in an apartment above the shop.

Not much is known about his life before 1892, when he graduated from high school and turned eighteen. That year, his father died in an accident. To help support his mother and an unmarried sister, Lewis found a job as a hauler in an Oshkosh furniture factory. He worked thirteen hours a day, six days a week, lugging heavy furniture around, and bringing home four dollars a week in wages.

In those days, a young man just out of high school was lucky to have a steady job. When the economic panic of 1893 swept across the country, Oshkosh was hit by hard times. Many workers lost their jobs. At some factories, grown men were replaced by children, who were paid lower wages.

A local newspaper protested:

> Even in these dull times, with the mills running about half time and with half a force, there are children working at many machines. The city is so full of idle men that when the street car company reduced the already slender pay of their drivers and brought on a strike, there were two or three applicants for each vacant space. And yet with an army of idle men in our midst, children who ought to be in school are doing factory work.
>
> This state of affairs is a disgrace to Oshkosh. The little work there is to be had should be done at decent wages and the little ones sent to school. Put men to work and let babies go home!

When Lewis's furniture factory went out of business, he had to look for other work. A quiet, scrawny youth, he cut and split firewood, delivered packages for a clothing store, and sold water filters from door to door. Finally, he was hired as a janitor by a bank. Eager to improve himself, he studied stenography at night and was promoted to work on the bank's books and act as secretary to the head cashier. "I was neither physically nor temperamentally fitted for any of these jobs," Hine said later.

His luck changed when he met Frank Manny, a professor of education at the State Normal School in Oshkosh, the local teachers' college. Manny encouraged Lewis to give up his bank job and take classes at the Normal School. At the age of twenty-five, Hine started college. He spent a year at the Normal School, then enrolled for another year at the University of Chicago, studying to be a teacher and working part-time to pay his expenses.

In 1901, Frank Manny was appointed superintendent of New York City's Ethical Culture School, which was famous for its progressive teaching methods. He invited Hine to go east with him and join the school's faculty as a teacher of geography and nature study. Hine jumped at the chance to live and work in the nation's biggest city. Besides teaching in New York, he continued his own studies, earning a master's degree in education at New York University. During the summer of 1904, he returned to Oshkosh to marry Sara Ann Rich, a former classmate.

At about that time, Hine took up photography. Frank Manny wanted someone to document school activities. Although Hine had never handled a camera in his life, Manny persuaded him to become the school photographer. Using a ten-dollar box camera, he began to photograph scenes of school life. He set up a darkroom and formed an after-school camera club, learning the art of photography along with his students.

Hine's photos of school activities proved so popular that Frank Manny decided to use photography as a teaching tool. At the time, millions of immigrants were pouring into the United States from every corner of Europe, especially from impoverished regions of eastern and southern Europe. Manny wanted his students to have the same regard for these newcomers as they had for the Pilgrims who had landed at Plymouth Rock. He suggested

Boys' shop at the Ethical Culture School, c. 1907.

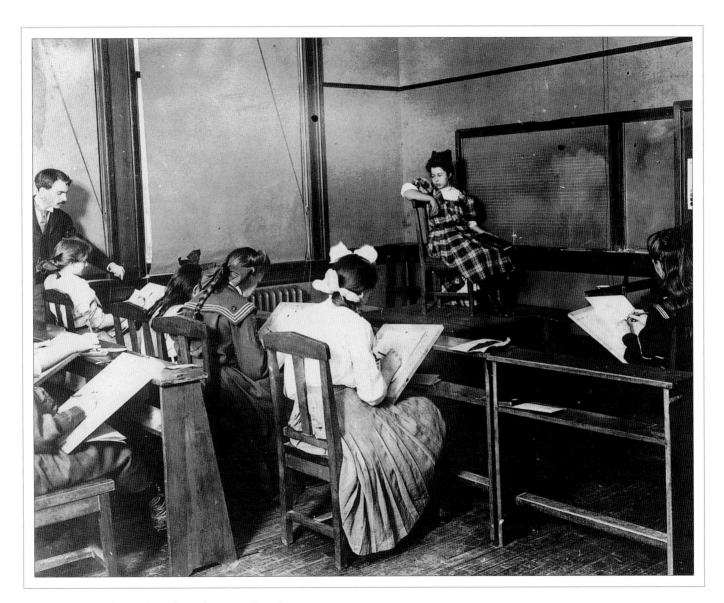

Art class at the Ethical Culture School, c. 1907.

that Hine take his camera to Ellis Island and photograph immigrant families as they arrived in the United States. In 1904, the two men made their first trip to Ellis Island together.

Called The Gateway to the New World, Ellis Island stood in New York Harbor within sight of the Statue of Liberty. Thousands of hopeful immigrants passed through the island's facilities every day. Clutching their baggage tickets, their name badges, and their children's hands, they stood in endless lines and waited anxiously in the crowded inspection hall. There they were questioned and examined and finally told whether they would be admitted to the United States or sent back to Europe.

Trailed by Manny, who helped carry and set up the camera equipment, Hine made his way through the surging crowds. In the midst of immigrants milling about, he picked out the people he wanted to photograph, set them apart from the crowd, and arranged the pose — almost always by means of sign language, since they did not speak English. Then, hoping they would not move away, he quickly set up his equipment. Later he wrote to a friend:

"Now, suppose we are elbowing our way through the mob at Ellis Island, trying to stop the surge of bewildered beings oozing through the corridors, up the stairs and all over the place, eager to get it all over and be on their way. Here is a small group that seems to have possibilities so we stop 'em and explain in pantomime that it would be lovely if they would only stick around just a moment. The rest of the human tide swirls around, often not

Immigrant family at Ellis Island, 1905.

Mother and child at Ellis Island, 1905.

too considerate of either the camera or us. We get the focus . . . then, hoping they will stay put, get the flash lamp ready."

Hine's equipment was somewhat outdated even by 1904 standards. He used a simple box-type 5 × 7–inch view camera, an old-fashioned bulb shutter, glass-plate negatives, and magnesium flash powder for illumination. He would set the camera on its rickety wooden tripod, focus the lens, insert the glass plate, dust his flashpan with powder, and with his own gestures and looks try to encourage the pose and expressions he wanted. Then he would raise the flashpan into the air and ignite the powder.

With a roar of flame and shower of sparks, the flashpan exploded. He opened the shutter at just the right moment, before the subjects closed their eyes against the blinding flash of the explosion.

Afterward, with a thick cloud of acrid smoke still hanging in the air, the immigrants would go on their way, and Hine would pack up his gear. One shot was all he had. There was no chance to make a second exposure.

Hine returned to Ellis Island many times during the next few years, taking about two hundred photographs in all. He went there as a man who took school pictures and left as a master photographer. The respect that he felt for his subjects, his direct and courteous manner when he approached them, allowed the immigrants to relax and be themselves when they faced his camera.

As his skill and confidence increased, he took on photographic assignments from the Child Welfare League, the National Consumers League, and the National Child Labor Committee. These reform groups were investigating living and working conditions in the teeming immigrant slums of New York and other big cities. They wanted photographs to document the abuses they were fighting to correct. Hine carried his camera into the streets, behind the closed doors of sweatshops that employed adults and children alike for long hours at low wages under miserable conditions. He climbed long flights of tenement stairs to gloomy one- and two-room apartments where whole families lived and worked.

One evening, he photographed a family of five as they sat at their kitchen table, making paper forget-me-nots by the light of a kerosene lamp. "Angelica is three years old," he reported. "She pulls apart the petals, inserts the center, and glues it to the stem, making 540 flowers a day for five cents."

Another family was making artificial roses when Hine visited their tenement apartment. "If they worked steadily from 8:00 in the morning until 8:00 or 9:00 at night, they could make 12 gross for $1.20," he wrote. " 'Flowers is cheap work now,' said the mother, 'too cheap work for anybody but us.' "

Working on these assignments, Hine was shaken by the poverty and hardship he witnessed. Photography gave him an opportunity to practice

Making artificial flowers in a New York tenement apartment.

Child in a doorway.

his belief in social justice and reform, and to express the compassion he felt for the underdog.

In 1908, the National Child Labor Committee offered him a full-time job as an investigative photographer in its campaign to outlaw child labor. Here was a chance to join one of the great causes of the time, to use his camera as a weapon against the exploitation of children. Hine resigned from his job at the Ethical Culture School, but at heart he remained a teacher. As he put it: "I felt that I was merely changing my educational efforts from the classroom to the world."

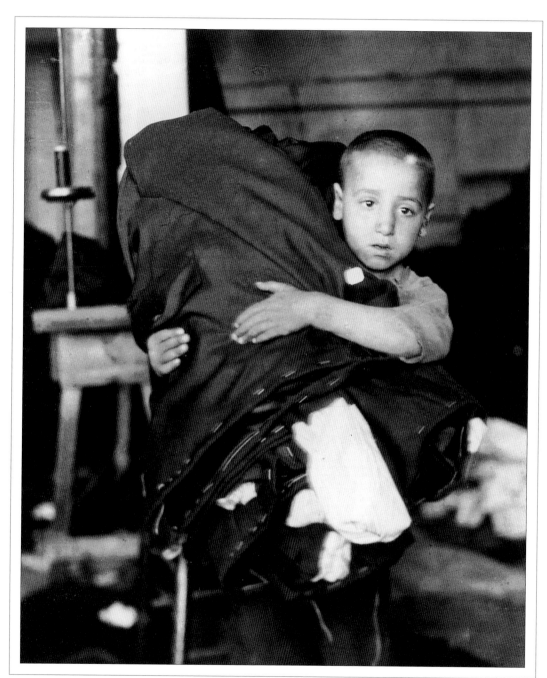

Leaving the factory with coats to be sewn at home, New York City, 1912.

CHAPTER THREE

SEEING
IS BELIEVING

Carrying a simple box camera like the one he used at Ellis Island, Lewis Hine traveled back and forth across the country, from the sardine canneries of Maine to the cotton fields of Texas. He took pictures of kids at work, listened to their stories, and reported on their lives.

His goal was to open the public's eyes to the horrors of child labor. He wanted to move people to action.

Hine wasn't concerned with children who worked at odd jobs after school or did chores around the house or the family farm. He didn't object to youngsters working as trainees and apprentices, learning skills they would use for the rest of their lives. The campaign against child labor was not directed against them. It was aimed at the exploitation of boys and girls as cheap labor.

"There is work that profits children, and there is work that brings profit only to employers," Hine said. "The object of employing children is not to train them, but to get high profits from their work."

Because children could be hired cheaply and were too small to complain, they were often employed to replace adult workers. In industries where large numbers of children were employed, their low wages pulled down the earnings of everyone else, so that grown-ups could not earn enough to support their families. As a result, poor families needed their children's wages just to survive.

Some people argued that child employees weren't really expected to work very hard. "Let me tell you right here," declared Hine, "that these [jobs] involve work, hard work, deadening in its monotony, exhausting physically . . . the worker's only joy [is getting paid]. We might even say of these children that they are condemned to work."

As criticism of child labor grew, a number of states passed laws regulating working hours and wages for children. But more often than not, those laws were filled with loopholes and favored the manufacturers. Some states failed to enforce even the weakest child-labor laws.

The National Child Labor Committee was fighting for strict laws and effective enforcement. Founded in 1904, it was a militant organization made up of men and women who believed that a healthy, happy, normal childhood was the rightful heritage of all children.

The NCLC wanted to ban the employment of children under fourteen years of age in most occupations, and under sixteen in dangerous trades like mining. For all children, the NCLC demanded an eight-hour day, no night work, and mandatory work permits based on documentary proof of age. The NCLC also wanted compulsory school-attendance laws, but it did not expend much effort on that seemingly impossible dream. It was tough enough to get honest child-labor laws passed and obeyed.

Young laundry worker, 1913.

Lewis Hine photographing children in a slum.

As Hine traveled, he discovered that investigating child labor was like entering an armed camp. Owners and managers regarded the little man with the big box camera as a troublemaker. Often they refused to let Hine into their plants. Angry foremen and factory police threatened him. In many places, child workers were kept out of sight, hidden from public view.

Leo, an eight-year-old doffer in a cotton mill,
Fayetteville, Tennessee, 1910.

To gain access to factories, mines, sweatshops, and mills, and to use his camera freely, Hine often had to disguise his real purpose. His students at the Ethical Culture School knew him as a talented actor and mimic. He would entertain them during nature walks by impersonating a wayward tramp or an itinerant peddler. Now he changed the roles he played, posing as a fire inspector, or an insurance salesman, or an industrial photographer who was after pictures of buildings and factory machinery.

In a textile mill, he would set up his camera to photograph a loom, then ask a child to stand next to the loom so that Hine could get a sense of scale, showing the size of the machinery. When the photograph was printed, it emphasized the fact that the worker who tended that loom was indeed a small child.

Whenever possible, Hine tried to photograph the workplace itself. If he couldn't do that, he waited at the factory gates with his fifty pounds of camera equipment, then photographed the young workers as they entered and left the plant. He reported from Augusta, Georgia: "Entrance to the mill was extremely difficult. The man in charge absolutely refused to let me through, even as a visitor. So I waited close outside the main gate, concealed in the darkness of the woods, and at 6:00 P.M. I counted about thirty-five boys who appeared to be from nine to fourteen years of age. I stopped them and took them around the corner for a flash-powder photo. Some of the smallest boys said they had been working at the mill for several years."

*Workers at an Augusta, Georgia, cotton mill pose for
a flash-powder photo outside the main gate.*

Knitting stockings in a hosiery mill, Loudon, Tennessee, 1910.

At the seafood cannery in Mississippi where five-year-old Manuel peeled shrimp, Hine was told that he would not be allowed to take pictures around the place during working hours. When he learned that the employees reported to work before dawn, hours before the manager arrived, Hine appeared at the cannery with his camera at five o'clock in the morning. Later that day, while the manager was eating lunch, Hine again photographed some young workers, this time from a rowboat he had landed at the cannery's wharf.

Since he often resorted to tricks in order to get the pictures he wanted, he was careful to document every photograph with precise facts and figures. Hine knew the height of each button on his vest from the floor, so he could measure a child standing alongside him with no one being the wiser. Hidden in his pocket was a small notebook. He used it to record the name, age, hours of work, daily earnings, schooling, and other facts about each child he photographed.

"All along I had to be double-sure that my photo data was 100% pure — no retouching or fakery of any kind," he wrote.

Young mill workers, Gastonia, North Carolina, 1908.

CHAPTER FOUR

SPINNERS, DOFFERS, AND SWEEPERS

Lewis Hine traveled constantly for the National Child Labor Committee, covering as many as fifty thousand miles a year by automobile and train. Sometimes he developed his glass-plate negatives in the cellars and coal bins of the rooming houses he stayed in.

His wife, Sara, accompanied him on several trips early in their marriage. In 1911, they traveled together through Mississippi and Virginia, where they collaborated on a report about "thirteen cotton mills, ten knitting mills, five silk mills, three woolen mills, and glass and shoe factories." Their only child, a boy named Corydon, was born the following year.

Hine found kids at work in every part of the country and in some of the nation's most important industries. Textile mills were big offenders, especially in the South, where one mill worker in every four was between the ages of ten and fifteen. No one knew how many workers were *younger* than ten, because they weren't counted.

Hine reported from North Carolina: "I found two little sisters spinning whose grandmother told me they were only six and seven years old. I found two boys under twelve whose hands had been mutilated in the mill. And I found any number of ten- and eleven-year-old children working an eleven-hour day (during the school term) at tasks involving eye strain and muscle strain. Is it any wonder, therefore, that I found a whole family, mother and five children, the oldest seventeen, of which not one could write his name?''

Throughout the segregated South, mill work was reserved for whites. Blacks were seldom hired. Most mill hands were impoverished white share-croppers and tenant farmers who had abandoned worn-out farms for the promise of steady employment in the mills.

Entire families left their farms to work in the mills. Many of the children quit school at an early age, or never went at all. Their parents, who often lacked an education themselves, didn't want their kids "wasting time" by attending school. They felt that youngsters should work to help support the family, just as they had worked earlier on the farm.

Children toiled in cotton mills as spinners, doffers, and sweepers. Girls were employed as spinners. They walked up and down long aisles, brushing lint from the machines and watching the whirling spools or bobbins for breaks in the cotton thread. When a break occurred, they had to mend it quickly by tying the ends together. A spinner tended six or eight "sides," as the long rows of spindles were called. She had to be on her feet nearly all the time, working eleven or twelve hours a day, six days a week.

View of the spinning room, Cornell Mill, Fall River, Massachusetts.

Sadie, a cotton mill spinner, Lancaster, South Carolina, 1908.

Hine described one spinner as "an emaciated little elf 50 inches high and weighing perhaps 48 pounds who works from 6 at night till 6 in the morning and who is so tiny that she had to climb up on the spinning frame to reach the top row of spindles."

Boys began working as doffers when they were seven or younger. It was their job to remove the whirling bobbins when they were filled with thread and replace them with empty ones. Many of the youngsters worked barefoot. That made it easier to climb onto the huge machines so they could reach the bobbins or broken threads. If they weren't careful, they could fall into the moving machinery or be caught by it. The accident rate for children working in the mills was twice as high as it was for adults.

In one mill, Hine reported, "A twelve-year-old doffer boy fell into a spinning machine and the unprotected gearing tore out two of his fingers. 'We don't have any accidents in this mill,' the overseer told me. 'Once in a while a finger is mashed or a foot, but it don't amount to anything.'"

The machinery made such a racket, workers had to shout to be heard above the din. And because heat and moisture helped keep the cotton threads from breaking, the mill windows were always kept closed. The hot, steamy air was filled with dust and lint that covered the workers' clothes and made it hard to breathe. Mill workers frequently developed tuberculosis, chronic bronchitis, and other respiratory diseases. A boy working in a cotton mill

A seven-year-old sweeper and a twelve-year-old doffer.

Climbing up on the machinery to replace bobbins.

was only half as likely to reach twenty years of age as a boy outside the mill. Girls had even less chance.

Textile-producing states that had enacted child-labor laws often failed to enforce them. "I cannot understand how it is that directors, superintendents, and other interested parties with ordinary eyes in their heads can see these tiny, immature children coming and going four times a day, and then say they do not have violations of the law," wrote Hine.

When a strong child-labor law was introduced in the Georgia state legislature in 1908, the state's mill owners made sure that the bill would be voted down. They produced long petitions from their workers, opposing the measure. On close examination, it was clear that hundreds of the signers could not even write their own names. Anyone could sign the petition simply by marking it with an X.

"Are you trying to do things for these people that they themselves do not want?" the mill owners asked. "Let them alone. They are happy."

Food canning was another industry that employed entire families, including young children. Hine visited seafood canneries and fruit and vegetable canneries in a dozen states, North and South. To his amazement, he found that kids who worked in the canning sheds were even younger than those in the cotton mills.

Cannery workers preparing beans, 1910.

Many cannery workers were recent immigrants from Europe. Every year, thousands of immigrant families were recruited in cities and shipped by train and boat to bleak cannery labor camps, where they remained until the canning season ended. Some of these camps were unfit to live in. Families were crowded into filthy, company-owned shacks that had no running water and were often infested with insects and rats.

School-age children left their city homes before the summer vacation began, and returned long after the fall term had started. They lagged far behind in their studies, if they attended school at all. Some of these immigrant children never learned English. They grew up wandering with their parents, moving from cannery to cannery, as they followed the seasons from strawberries and peaches in the North to oysters and shrimp in the South.

Work in the canning sheds began long before daybreak. "Come out with me to one of these canneries at 3 o'clock in the morning," Hine wrote from Mississippi. "Here is the crude, shedlike building, with a long dock at which the oyster boats unload their cargo. Near the dock is the ever-present shell pile, a monument to the patient work of little fingers. It is cold, damp, dark. The whistle blew some time ago, and the young workers slipped into meagre garments, snatched a bite to eat, and hurried to the shucking shed. . . . Boys and girls, six, seven, and eight years old, take their places with the adults and work all day."

Oyster shuckers at work, Dunbar, Louisiana, 1911.

Four-year-old Mary shucks two pots of oysters a day,
Dunbar, Louisiana, 1911.

Parents wanted their kids working at their sides, so they could keep an eye on them. Since there was no place to leave the children, even the youngest and the newborn were taken to the cannery sheds every day. On winter mornings, infants wrapped in blankets slept in baby carriages and boxes next to warm packing-house stoves. Toddlers wandered about the sheds, playing among the shells and imitating their parents. As soon as they were big enough to handle a knife, they were "allowed to help." Parents desperately needed the money their children could earn.

Boys and girls stood side by side with the grown-ups, picking up clusters of oyster shells, prying them open, and dropping the meat into pails. When a pail was filled, it was carried off to be weighed. For a pail that held four pounds of shelled oysters, the worker received five cents. Children usually filled one or two pails a day, adults eight or nine.

The rough, sharp oyster shells were hard on little fingers, but raw shrimp were far worse. As the shrimp were peeled, they oozed an acid so strong, it ate holes in workers' leather shoes and even in the tin pails they used. Children with swollen, bleeding fingers were a common sight. At night, they soaked their fingers in an alum solution to harden their skin and help heal their wounds.

The shucking of oysters and peeling of shrimp went on for hours without a break until the day's supply was disposed of, usually by late afternoon.

Seven-year-old Rosie, an experienced oyster shucker,
Bluffton, South Carolina, 1913.

In fruit and vegetable canneries, the hours were even longer during the peak of the season. Using sharp knives, children husked corn, snipped off the ends of beans, and peeled apples and tomatoes. Sometimes a knife slipped, cutting a finger to the bone.

Cannery owners claimed that all family members were needed, because fresh produce was highly perishable and had to be canned quickly. How about the children? Hine asked. Aren't they perishable?

*Young West
Virginia coal miner.*

CHAPTER FIVE

BREAKER BOYS

Lewis Hine took some of his most haunting photos in the dark tunnels and grimy breaker rooms of the nation's coal mines. In Pennsylvania, the biggest coal-producing state, thousands of fourteen- and fifteen-year-old boys were employed legally in the mines. At the same time, thousands of younger boys, some of them only nine or ten, worked illegally. The state's child-labor law was almost useless, since it required no binding proof of a worker's age.

Boys worked in a variety of jobs — as mule drivers, couplers, runners, spraggers, and gate tenders. Most of the younger boys were employed in the coal breakers outside the mines. Their faces black with soot, they sat in rows on wooden boards placed over coal chutes. As coal came pouring through the chutes, the boys bent over, reached down, and picked out pieces of slate and stone that could not burn.

They had to watch carefully, since coal and slate look so much alike. If

Breaker boys at work, South Pittston, Pennsylvania, 1911.

a boy reached too far and slipped into the coal that was constantly flowing beneath him, he could be mangled or killed. "While I was there, two breaker boys fell or were carried into the coal chute, where they were smothered to death," Hine reported from a Pennsylvania mine.

A foreman armed with a broom handle stood in front of the breaker room. He watched the boys as intently as they watched the moving coal. He used the broom handle to rap the heads and shoulders of those who, in his opinion, were not working hard enough. Hine wrote: "The pieces rattled down through the long chutes at which the breaker boys sat. It's like sitting in a coal bin all day long, except that the coal is always moving and clattering and cuts their fingers. Sometimes the boys wear lamps in their caps to help them see through the thick dust. They bend over the chutes until their backs ache, and they get tired and sick because they have to breathe coal dust instead of good, pure air."

Many of the breaker boys suffered from chronic coughs. "There are twenty boys in that breaker," one of the foremen said, "and I bet you could shovel fifty pounds of coal dust out of their systems."

When the boys turned twelve, they began to work down in the mines, where there was always the threat of cave-ins and explosions. One of Hine's photos shows a trapper or door boy sitting on a bench in front of a heavy wooden door. The picture was taken with a flashpan five hundred feet down the mine shaft and three-quarters of a mile underground from there. It was this boy's job to open the door when a coal car came through, and then close the door quickly to keep air from blowing through the mine and lowering the temperature.

"A lonely job," wrote Hine, "by himself nine or ten hours a day in absolute

Noon hour in the coal breaker.

darkness save for his little oil lamp. . . . Owing to the intense darkness in the mine, I didn't notice the chalk drawings on the door until I had developed the photographic plate. These drawings tell the tale of the boy's loneliness underground."

Vance, a trapper boy in a West Virginia coal mine, 1908.

The only proof of age required for mine workers in Pennsylvania, and most other mining states, was a statement signed by the boy's parents. And yet court hearings revealed the true ages of those boys who became victims of mine disasters.

One youngster, a lad named Patrick Kearny, lost his life in a mine accident in 1907. At an inquest following his death, the foreman testified that the company had a certificate stating that Patrick was fourteen, even though he appeared to be only about ten years old. He was "kind of a small boy," the foreman said, "but I thought he might be older than he looked." In any

LAD FELL TO DEATH IN BIG COAL CHUTE

Dennis McKee Dead and Arthur Allbecker Had Leg Burned In the Lee Mines.

Falling into a chute at the Chauncey colliery of the George S. Lee Coal Company at Avondale, this afternoon, Dennis McKee, aged 15, of West Nanticoke, was smothered to death and Arthur Allbecker, aged 15, had both of his legs burned and injured. Dr. Biel, of Plymouth, was summoned and dressed the burns of the injured boy.

He was removed to his home at Avondale.

Both boys were employed as breaker boys, and going too close to the chutes fell in. Fellow workmen rushed to their assistance and soon had them out of the chutes. When taken out McKee was found to be dead. His remains were removed to his home at West Nanticoke. Allbecker will recover.

News item,
Wilkes-Barre News,
January 7, 1911.

Lewis Hine emerging from a coal mine with his camera equipment.

case, since Patrick's parents had signed the work certificate, there was no need to question it.

Afterward, Patrick's father was called to testify. He admitted that the boy had been born in June 1898. He was only nine and a half when he died. His father had signed the certificate stating that Patrick was fourteen because he wanted to get work for the boy.

"It was very scary, believe me," said a veteran miner, recalling his boyhood days in the mines. "Really, I don't know how in the world I got the nerve to go there in the first place. You didn't dare say anything. You didn't dare quit, because it was something to have a job — at eight cents an hour!"

Glass making was another industry that employed thousands of boys in tough and dangerous jobs. Most of these youngsters worked as blowers' assistants in glassworks furnace rooms. The intense heat and glaring light of the open furnaces, where the glass was kept in a molten state, could cause eye trouble, lung ailments, heat exhaustion, and a long list of other medical problems.

The temperature of molten glass is 3,133 degrees Fahrenheit. The temperature in the glass factories ranged between 100 and 130 degrees. Fumes and dust hung in the air. Broken glass littered the floors. It wasn't surprising that cuts and burns were the most common injuries.

Workers were paid by the piece, so they had to keep moving fast for

Glass factory worker, Alexandria, Virginia, 1911.

Tending the furnace in a glass factory, Morgantown, West Virginia, 1908.

hours at a time without a break. A typical glassblower's assistant made about sixty-five cents a day.

Since the furnaces were kept burning continuously, glass factories operated around the clock. Many of the boys were required to work at night. Often, they faced a transportation problem. The night shift started at 5:00 P.M. and ended at 3:00 A.M., when there was no streetcar service. A boy had the choice of a nap on the factory floor until five or six o'clock, when the cars started running, or a long walk home in the dark. In winter, this meant a sudden change from the hot air inside the factory to the frigid air outside.

Because of these unhealthy and hazardous work conditions, employees in the glass-making industry at that time had a life expectancy of only forty-one to forty-two years.

Factory owners claimed that they couldn't operate without the labor of young boys, that workers over sixteen were too slow and clumsy to perform the boys' work. And yet most adult glassworks employees refused to let their own kids follow them into the factories. As one longtime worker put it: "I would rather send my boys straight to hell than send them by way of the glass house."

*Sixth Street Market,
Cincinnati, Ohio,
10:00 P.M., August 22,
1908.*

CHAPTER SIX

STREET KIDS AND FARM KIDS

People were often shocked and outraged when they saw photos of young children working in mines, factories, and mills. And yet children the same age, hard at work on city streets, attracted little attention.

Working children were seen everywhere in America's cities. They sold newspapers, shined shoes, ran errands, delivered packages, hauled firewood, coal, and ice, and labored in sweatshops. People passing by took it for granted that a kid at work on the street was helping to support a widowed mother or an ailing parent.

Some of these children were in business for themselves. Kids peddled flowers, shoelaces, ribbons, and candy from boxes set up on street corners. Young bootblacks carrying homemade shoeshine kits watched for customers in train stations and city parks. Newsboys and an occasional newsgirl hawked their papers from curbs and corners, shouting, "Extra! Extra! Read all about it!" Some of the youngsters photographed by Lewis Hine had been selling newspapers on street corners since they were six or seven years old.

These "newsies" received no salary or commission. They paid cash for each armload of newspapers, and took the loss for any papers they couldn't sell. Groups of newsies gathered at newspaper offices in the middle of the night, waiting for the early-morning editions to roll off the presses. Then each of them staked out a territory that was forbidden to others.

Child-labor reformers did not object to kids delivering newspapers to subscribers before or after school, or working at other part-time jobs. But they were strongly opposed to youngsters working in unregulated jobs on city streets at all hours of the day and night.

Many of these street kids lived in poverty, never went to school, and had no real home. In New York City alone, thousands of homeless working children — orphans and runaways — lived in shelters run by the Children's Aid Society. For a few cents a day, a child could pay for a dormitory bunk, a breakfast of bread and coffee, and a supper of pork and beans. The society operated five lodging houses for boys in New York, and one for girls.

Children who worked as peddlers, bootblacks, and newsies were looked upon as "little merchants." People liked to think of them as enterprising youngsters starting out on the road to success. Like the heroes of so many popular dime novels of the time, kids could work their way from rags to riches.

New York City newsboys photographed near the Brooklyn Bridge at 1:00 on a Sunday morning, 1906.

Newsgirls in Wilmington, Delaware, 1910.

Bootblack, Third Avenue and Ninth Street, New York City, 1910.

It was true that some successful men had started out as newsboys. But many others who began the same way found themselves at a dead end. They faced a bleak future, their prospects dimmed by their lack of education and skills.

During the early 1900s, when many crops were still planted and harvested by hand, more children worked on farms than in any other occupation. People who opposed child labor in industry often felt differently about farming. Who could argue against wholesome, healthful outdoor work? Children labored in the fresh air beside their parents, learning useful farming skills and valuable lessons in family cooperation.

Unfortunately, these widely held beliefs about the joys of farm work did not always correspond to harsh facts. True enough, some youngsters did work on old-fashioned family farms. But many others were nothing more than hired hands who traveled from farm to farm with their families, performing the same backbreaking labor as did their mothers and fathers.

None of the child-labor laws in effect at that time applied to farm work. Farm workers had no protection. In agriculture, any child could work at any age under any conditions for any number of hours a day or week.

Entire families labored in the fields, including three- and four-year-old kids. Some families spent the year following the crops, seldom staying in one place for more than a few weeks at a time. Others lived in the city

Cotton-pickers ranging in age from five to nine, Bells, Texas, 1913.

Hine saw "tiny bits of humanity picking cotton in every field." Some of these children had been brought in from nearby orphanages. Others were migrants who worked in family groups. All of them picked cotton from sunup to sundown.

A four-year-old girl told Hine that she picked eight pounds of cotton a day, while her five-year-old sister picked thirty pounds, adding to the family's meager income. "The sunshine in the cotton fields has blinded our eyes to the monotony, overwork, and hopelessness in their lives," wrote Hine.

On a trip to Colorado, Hine interviewed families who worked in the sugar-beet fields. During summer hoeing, children, like adults, bent over clumps of plants, digging for hours. In the fall, the mature beets were pulled from the ground and "topped." Topping required holding a beet against the knee and slicing off the top with a sixteen-inch knife that had a sharp prong at one end. Accidents happened all too often. "I hooked my knee with the beet knife," a seven-year-old boy told Hine, "but I just went on working."

It wasn't unusual to see children with badly chapped hands pulling and topping beets in the middle of November, as cold winds blew across the fields and ice formed in the furrows. During a late harvest, when a heavy frost was expected, everyone worked far into the night by lantern light. "We all work fourteen hours a day at times," a father told Hine, "because when the beets is ready, they has to be done."

Pulling beets near Sterling, Colorado, 1915.

Topping beets with a hooked knife.

A raveler and a looper in a hosiery mill, Loudon, Tennessee, 1910.

CHAPTER SEVEN

MAKING A DIFFERENCE

I am sure I am right in my choice of work," Lewis Hine told his old friend Frank Manny. "My child labor photos have already set the authorities to work to see if such things can be possible."

People all over the country saw Hine's photographs in newspapers and magazines, and in a steady stream of publications sent out by the National Child Labor Committee. The photos publicized what many had refused to believe. They stood as graphic evidence that industrial America was exploiting its children. "These pictures speak for themselves," the NCLC declared, "and prove that the law is being violated."

Hine personally designed pamphlets, booklets, and photo exhibits on child labor. He wrote descriptive captions for each photo, experimenting with the most effective ways to combine pictures and words. To describe this new format that he was developing, he coined the term "photo-story."

Some of his best photos were made into stereopticon slides for use at illustrated lectures. The NCLC loaned sets of slides to local groups and organizations, along with a typewritten talk. Hine himself lectured on child labor wherever the committee sent him. As he spoke, the slides were projected on a screen. The children's faces, bright and luminous in the darkness of the auditorium, held his audience spellbound as he described the hardships the children endured.

A newspaper reporter who saw an exhibit of Hine's photos at a conference in Birmingham, Alabama, was stunned by the power of the images. He wrote:

> There has been no more convincing proof of the absolute necessity of child labor laws . . . than these pictures showing the suffering, the degradation, the immoral influence, the utter lack of anything that is wholesome in the lives of these poor little wage earners. They speak far more eloquently than any [written] work — and depict a state of affairs which is terrible in its reality — terrible to encounter, terrible to admit that such things exist in civilized communities.

Hine's photos were meant to shock and anger those who saw them. They were intended to mobilize public opinion, and that is exactly what they did. The photos became a powerful weapon in the crusade against child labor.

A greaser in a coal mine carrying two pails of grease, Bessie Mine, Alabama, 1910.

Hine's job as an investigative photographer for the National Child Labor Committee lasted about ten years. In 1918, he accepted a special assignment from the American Red Cross. He went overseas and traveled for several months through the ruined lands of war-torn Europe, photographing refugees and relief efforts in the aftermath of World War I.

Refugee mother and child, 1918.

Paris, 1918.

Worker at a dynamo, 1921.

Lewis Hine playing tennis, c. 1927.

an assignment or sell his photographs that year was unsuccessful. Unable to make his mortgage payments, he was about to lose his comfortable home in Hastings-on-Hudson, just north of New York City, where he had lived since 1918.

He tried to get a foundation grant for a new project — a photographic study of foreign-born Americans, their lives at home and at work. When he was turned down, he was forced to apply for public assistance. The man who had photographed the poor and the exploited with so much compassion and courage now found himself standing at the end of a relief line. "The Hine fortunes are at an all-time low," he told a friend.

Even then, a revival of interest in Hine's work was beginning to surface. A small group of young photographers and critics had rediscovered Lewis Hine. Some of them wrote articles praising him as a pioneer of documentary photography. *Life* magazine bought some of his "old treasures." CBS asked him to prepare a series of radio broadcasts about the working man. And in 1939, a major exhibition of Hine's photographs opened at the Riverside Museum in New York.

The show lifted Hine's spirits, but the recognition came too late. That year, the bank foreclosed on Hine's home. Soon afterward, on Christmas morning, 1939, his wife, Sara, died after a lingering illness. Hine survived her by less than a year. He passed away after an operation on November 4, 1940, at the age of sixty-six, when he was still hoping to find sponsors for future projects.

About two years before his death, Hine befriended a twenty-one-year-old fledgling photographer named Walter Rosenblum. They met at the Photo League in New York. Despite his own difficulties, Hine tutored the younger man, recommended him for free-lance work, and wrote a letter of introduction that said, "Here is a new and better Hine."

"I always sought his company . . . and I was soon completely under his spell," Rosenblum recalled. "We spent many hours in quiet conversation. I felt embraced by his presence. There were no formalities with Hine, no status games — just honesty and simple dignity. I had never met anyone like him."

Lewis Hine died in poverty, neglected by all but a few. But his reputation continued to grow, and he is recognized today as a master American photographer. His photographs have become part of our national memory. They remind us what it was like to be a child and to labor like an adult, at a time when most labor was far harsher than it is now.

Through his camera, a young spinner in a Carolina cotton mill gazes at us across a distance of eighty years. In her eyes we can still see the pain and cruelty of child labor, but Hine also captured her humanity, dignity, and strength.

A friend once asked why his kids seemed so beautiful, and he said, "I only photograph beautiful children."

Certainly, he had a way with children. With a smile and a few kind words, a touch of his hand, he let them know that he was their friend and ally. He

Mill girl.

Mill boy.

saw the beauty that resides in every child, and kids responded by trusting themselves to his camera.

Hine's images of working children stirred America's conscience and helped change the nation's laws. With his box camera and his sympathetic eye, he made a dramatic difference in people's lives. In a real sense, the face of America never looked the same again.

BY THE CHILDREN OF AMERICA IN MINES AND

FACTORIES AND WORKSHOPS ASSEMBLED

WHEREAS, We, Children of America, are declared to have been born free and equal, and

WHEREAS, We are yet in bondage in this land of the free; are forced to toil the long day or the long night, with no control over the conditions of labor, as to health or safety or hours or wages, and with no right to the rewards of our service, therefore be it

RESOLVED, I — That childhood is endowed with certain inherent and inalienable rights, among which are freedom from toil for daily bread; the right to play and to dream; the right to the normal sleep of the night season; the right to an education, that we may have equality of opportunity for developing all that there is in us of mind and heart.

RESOLVED, II — That we declare ourselves to be helpless and dependent; that we are and of right ought to be dependent, and that we hereby present the appeal of our helplessness that we may be protected in the enjoyment of the rights of childhood.

RESOLVED, III — That we demand the restoration of our rights by the abolition of child labor in America.

NATIONAL CHILD LABOR COMMITTEE, 1913

Lewis Hine.

CHILD LABOR THEN AND NOW

When Lewis Hine took his earliest photos for the National Child Labor Committee, the employment of young children in factories, mines, streets, and fields was commonplace in America. Some states did have child-labor laws, but for the most part, those laws were weak and enforcement was lax. There were no generally accepted standards to protect working children from exploitation.

Progress came slowly, and only after a long and bitter struggle. The establishment of the United States Children's Bureau in 1912 marked a critical breakthrough. This government agency was charged with investigating working conditions and mobilizing public opinion against child labor. Thanks to the campaign waged by the NCLC, and to Lewis Hine's persuasive photographs, a growing number of Americans had come to believe that the federal government should be actively concerned with children's welfare — and the government had responded.

From then on, reformers focused their efforts on Congress and the courts as they fought for a national child-labor law that would apply equally to all American children. Congress passed such laws in 1916 and again in 1918, but the Supreme Court declared them unconstitutional because they infringed on states' rights and "denied children the freedom to contract work." In 1924, Congress passed a constitutional amendment that would authorize a national child-labor law. That measure was killed by groups that opposed any increase in federal power in areas related to children. Their lobbying kept many states from ratifying the amendment, and after ten years, it died.

Child labor began to disappear only during the Great Depression of the 1930s, a period of high unemployment, when adults competed for even the lowest-paying jobs held by children. At the same time, determined opposition to child labor by increasingly powerful labor unions, along with industry's growing needs for a better-educated work force, gradually diminished the role of child labor.

Federal regulation of child labor did not succeed until 1938, when President Franklin Delano Roosevelt signed the Fair Labor Standards Act, which set minimum wage and maximum hour standards for all workers in interstate commerce, and also placed limitations on child labor. In effect, the employment of children under sixteen was prohibited in manufacturing and mining. Congress amended the law in 1949 to include businesses not covered

Edith, five years old.

Mart, five years old.

earlier — principally, commercial agriculture, transportation, communications, and public utilities. In other occupations, federal laws prohibit children under sixteen from working during school hours and limit the number of hours they can work after school and on weekends.

Compared to conditions in 1904, when the National Child Labor Committee was founded, gratifying progress has been made. Still, child labor has not vanished from America. It exists today among the children of recent immigrants who toil next to their mothers behind the closed doors of sweatshops; among a half-million poverty-wracked children of migrant farm workers; among hundreds of thousands of youngsters who hold jobs prohibited by law, or who work excessive hours while attending school.

The NCLC is still carrying out its mission to combat violations of the child-labor laws, and to promote the rights and dignity of children and youth. Every year since 1985, the Committee has presented the Lewis Hine Awards, recognizing the accomplishments of dedicated men and women who, like Hine himself, have helped change the lives of young people across the country.

CURTIS, VERNA POSEVER, and STANLEY MALLACH. *Photography and Reform: Lewis Hine and the National Child Labor Committee.* Milwaukee: Milwaukee Art Museum, 1984.

DOHERTY, JONATHAN L., ed. *Women at Work: 153 Photographs by Lewis W. Hine.* New York: Dover Publications in association with George Eastman House, 1981.

GOLDBERG, VICKI. *The Power of Photography: How Photographs Changed Our Lives.* New York: Abbeville Press, 1991.

GUTMAN, JUDITH MARA. *Lewis W. Hine and the American Social Conscience.* New York: Walker and Company, 1967.

————. *Lewis W. Hine: Two Perspectives.* New York: Grossman Publishers, 1974.

HINE, LEWIS W. *Men at Work: Photographic Studies of Modern Men and Machines.* New York: Macmillan, 1932. Reprint. New York: Dover Publications and the International Museum of Photography at George Eastman House, 1977.

KAPLAN, DAILE, ed. *Photo Story: Selected Letters and Photographs of Lewis W. Hine.* Washington, D.C.: Smithsonian Institution Press, 1992.

KEMP, JOHN R., ed. *Lewis Hine: Photographs of Child Labor in the New South.* Jackson, Mississippi: University Press of Mississippi, 1986.

ROSENBLUM, NAOMI, WALTER ROSENBLUM, and ALAN TRACHTENBERG. *America and Lewis Hine.* New York: Aperture, 1977.

TRATTNER, WALTER I. *Crusade for the Children: A History of the National Child Labor Committee and Child Labor Reform in America.* New York: Quadrangle Books, 1970.

FILM:

America and Lewis Hine. A film by Nina Rosenblum and Daniel V. Allentuck. New York: The Cinema Guild, 1984.

For a comprehensive bibliography of articles and photo stories by Lewis Hine and articles about him through 1976, see Rosenblum *et al.*, *America and Lewis Hine.*

The author is grateful to the following people for their help and encouragement: Dorrie Bernstein, National Child Labor Committee; Stephen Daiter, Stephen Daiter Books, Chicago; James C. Giblin; Janet Hirschfeld, Ethical Culture School; Daile Kaplan, Swann Galleries, New York; Janice Madhu, George Eastman House, Rochester, New York.

The photographs in this book, with the exception of those in which Hine appears, are by Lewis Hine, are from the following sources, and are used with permission:

Ethical Culture School: 10, 11

George Eastman House: vi, 6, 23, 24, 28, 42, 44, 53, 74, 75, 76, 78, 79, 80, 82, 83, 84, 96, 98

Lewis W. Hine Collection, United States History, Local History and Genealogy Division, The New York Public Library, Astor, Lenox & Tilden Foundations: 4, 13, 14, 18, 61, 64, 66, 68, 69, 92, 95

Library of Congress: frontispiece, vii, 3, 17, 25, 30, 33, 34, 36, 37, 39, 46, 48, 50, 51, 52, 55, 56, 62, 70, 73, 87

National Archives: 41, 58, 88

National Child Labor Committee: 20, 27, 90

INDEX

Page numbers in *italics* indicate photos